On the day Lam went missing, Katie Orphan, who owns a book store named "The Last Bookstore", recalls talking to Elisa. "…Talking about, you know, what books she was getting and whether or not what she was getting would be too heavy for her to carry around as she travelled, or take home with her". Katie then went on to say that Lam had bought gifts for her parents and sister. Nothing more was said about this interaction, so perhaps this cannot be used to assess Lam's physical or mental state at that time.

The Investigation:

On February 6th the Los Angeles police department went public in their efforts to seek help in locating Elisa Lam, and fliers containing her picture, were distributed around the internet and surrounding areas. A week later, they released a video that shows Lam acting peculiarly, in what was discovered to be the last footage of her alive. Although it was instrumental in the search for Elisa, it is not actually known what date and time the video was recorded- but we do know that it as sometime around the 31st January, and the 1st February.

During the investigation and attempts to find Elisa, the LA police department searched all parts of the hotel that the law would allow. Police sniffer dogs were sent into the hotel, to try and detect Elisa's scent, but to no avail. The police then went on to divulge that they could not legally search all rooms in the hotel, because it was not confirmed that a crime had indeed taken place. On February 19th, a hotel worker went up onto the roof of the Cecil Hotel, to investigate poor water pressure, that some of the guests had been complaining of. This is where he found Elisa Lam's dead body, floating in one of the water tanks on the roof. Before we can investigate this case further, and analyse theories and suggestions, we shall first look at Elisa as a person, and her background.

About Elisa:

Although it may not have seemed it to anyone who had passing contact with Elisa, but she was clearly a very complex, and some would say troubled individual.

What seems bizarre is that Randy Schmidt, who is associated with the University of British Columbia (where Lam studied), said that Lam had attended classes up until August, but not at all in the year of her death. Does this mean she had a hidden agenda that her parents were unaware of, as her family said they believed that she had been attending all of her classes up to her leaving to travel and ultimately, her death? Schmidt then said "Unfortunately, we do not have much more to say, other than to extend our deepest sympathies to the family" Every person that had dealings with Elisa spoke fondly of

4

her. Another person who met Elisa, when she was travelling before arriving in LA, was Teika Steins- the manager of a hotel in Toronto, Canada, where Lam stayed earlier on in her travels. Steins impression of her was that she was "friendly and outgoing".

Elisa's family were very close-knit, and Lam was in contact with them without fail, everyday. The family owned and ran a restaurant in Burnaby, British Columbia. Flowers were left here following the finding of her body. The restaurant was also temporarily closed, in respect of her death. A lady who works nearby the restaurant, Tanya Grohmann, said that she was "saddened by the loss" and on speaking about the family she commented "They are a hardworking family. They immigrated here. They have been in the neighbourhood for nine years working. They are honest people". Knowing how respected Lam and her family were, not only in their community but wider afield, makes this whole case even more tragic.

A further statement regarding Elisa's character came from her long term neighbour Edward Jiang. He said that "She's a good girl, I hope she is ok" (This came during the period where Lam was missing, before her body was found, hence its present tense). Elisa had a best friend named Mai Vo, who upon viewing the video of Lam in the elevator, said that it was "unlike Lam" and her view was that Lam had been drugged. It was also her opinion that Lam had been a happy-go-lucky type of person, then went on to reiterate that Lam was travelling alone and that her trip was only intended to last two or three months.

Was she mentally ill?

Some people believed that Elisa was suffering mental health issues (we shall go into this in more detail later on), and others contend this. However, her sister Sara Lam said that she did indeed have a history of bipolar disorder and depression. She then went on to say that Elisa was taking four prescribed medications at the time of her death- wellbutrin, lamotrigine, quetiapine and another, which she could not recall. Sara said that her sister did not have any suicidal ideations or suicide attempts that she knew of.

It is hard to identify what type of emotions Lam was feeling at the time of her disappearance, because few people report seeing her around that time, and the only real evidence we have to utilise is the video of her in the elevator. Analysing the video step by step, her actions suggest her moods were fluctuating and whilst in the elevator she bizarrely seems to be indicating a whole range of different emotions- confidence, joy and fear being a few of those. It could be said that she was

6

perhaps playing a form of hide and seek....but who was the hider and who was the seeker?

It is clear that Elisa wrote many blogs before, and during her travels, spanning over a number of years. She continued to update her blog even up to the time of her death. On the date of her checking into the Cecil Hotel, Lam wrote the following in her blog: "I'm going out tonight. I really hope no creeper comes near me. Seriously though those Italian and Mexican guys go after you STRONG. Show the slightest inclination and they hound you". The following day she posts that she lost her cell phone. It would appear that Lam's friend "Amanda" was sent a postcard, by Lam that mentioned "something shocking". No further details were given by Amanda, and the postcard has never been seen or found, so it allows the imagination to wonder. Before we can speculate further, we must first analyse the footage of Elisa in the elevator prior to her death.

The Elevator Footage:

The footage of Elisa Lam in one of the Cecil Hotels two elevators was recorded sometime on February 1st. The video was released by the local police department on February 14th, as the hunt for Lam stepped up a level. The case was to become more mystifying after its release.

The video is around two and a half minutes long. It has been greatly scrutinised due to Elisa's strange behaviour inside the elevator. Unfortunately, some people believe that the video had been tampered with prior to its public release. The reasons being, that the video is abnormally grainy and the time stamp is inexplicably blurred and unreadable. Some people also speculate that the area around Lam's mouth is somewhat bleary and that parts of the video clip had been slowed down, or removed altogether.

Firstly, Elisa walks into the lift, wearing a sweater, t-shirt, shorts and sandals. At this point she does not look fearful, and has a relaxed gait. She walks immediately to the button panel and presses numerous floors before moving backwards to the corner. When the door fails to close she peers out of the door and looks around, before moving back into the elevator. The door remains open, and so Lam once again moves over to the button panel. Her feet and arms remain neutral, again not indicating fear. Lam then moves over and stands for several moments in the doorway, then oddly moves into the hallway (which is partially visible due to the camera's positioning). She looks to one side, re-enters the elevator, looks again to the side, and back out of the doorway. For a few brief seconds we lose sight of her almost completely, as she is covered behind the wall- at this point, the elevator door continues to stay open.

From here, Elisa's behaviour becomes even more peculiar. She moves an arm to her head and comes back into the elevator, and then places both of her hands onto the sides of the still open door. Strangely she moves to the button panel once again, and presses numerous buttons (some of the buttons are pressed more than once, for unknown reasons). Putting her hands over her ears, she re-enters the elevator and moves to the back wall, where she had previously been standing. Elisa then turns and rubs her forearms together, then waves out her hands to her side, spreading out her fingers and rocking slightly as she does this. The door at last closes, as Lam backs against the wall, before walking out to the left.

Up until the point of Lam retreating back into the elevator, her body language does not indicate that she was in fear or afraid. When she moves back to the left front corner however, she moves her feet close together and while this does not suggest that she is afraid, it is the type of body language associated with anxiety and low confidence. Bizarrely Lam moves her elbows out laterally exposing her arm pits and preens her hair. It is agreed by body language specialists that this deliberately slow movement is a strong reliable indicator of "sexual interest". They concur that she may be thinking about, or maybe visually seeing, a person of interest.

Further scrutiny of the footage show that her movements slow further- was she feeling light headed or experiencing extremes of emotion? At some point we see Lam smile- but it may well have been a forced or "untrue" smile. Later on in the video we see many non-verbal indicators- her body language is that of a person taking part in conversation (with a person out of view), or possibly an upcoming interaction. Numerous times Lam's feet go onto her toes and this is a well known marker of a person experiencing happiness, joy and optimism.

If the video was found to have occurred just before Elisa's death it could be a strong possibility that whoever, or whatever Elisa is interacting with may have contributed to or have knowledge of Lam's death.

Due to its peculiarity, when posted on the internet, the video soon got many millions of reviews and comments. Some people's comments suggested that the video was chilling to watch, and one person even said "I'm so scared...shaking...I'm numb". There are countless theories surrounding this strange video. One of the factors that led to the finding of Elisa's body was that the poor water supply being supplied to the hotel's residents was being questioned.

Clearly, when Elisa went missing, one of the last places anyone would choose to look or investigate would be the ten foot tall water tanks on the roof of the hotel she was staying in. It plainly wasn't the most obvious place to look, however the police did briefly go onto the roof, but did not open the hefty lids of any of the four water tanks that were situated there.

Andrew Smith, of LAPD, said during an interview, that the tanks have hinged lids, but he believes that when officers went onto the roof, all four lids were shut, and "they didn't think someone would climb up, or go onto that lid". When the body was found, Smith initially said that he didn't know if she was floating on the top or at the bottom of the tank. But a body at the bottom of the tank would be difficult to see" Either way, we know that shortly past 10am, on the morning of Feb 19, 2013, Elisa Lam's body was found in one of the tanks atop the roof.

The reason the tanks were checked, was because guests were complaining of problems with the water in the hotel. Though these complaints were shunned initially, after around three weeks, it was decided that a hotel maintenance worker should go and check the tanks (at this point, they openly did not think that they would find anything amiss).

The contaminated water supply:

CNN stated that the hotel guests complained about the water having a "funny taste". Yet they continued to bathe in it, drink it, and brush their teeth with it. They did this for just short of three weeks, whilst unbeknown to everyone, Elisa's body was slowly decomposing in one of the water tanks that supplied the water to the guests.

On of the guests, Sabrina Baugh, said "The water did have a funny taste". She, along with her husband, carried on using the water for eight days. She goes on to say "We never thought anything of it; we thought it was just the way it was here. The shower was awful, when you turn the tap on, the water was coming black for the first two seconds, and then it was back to normal". Michael Baugh, said "Knowing now what they didn't know then about the water is sickening. It makes you feel literally physically sick, but more than that you feel it psychologically. You think about it and it is not good". Another patron, Annette Suzuki stated "I was using the water for, you know, washing my hands, drinking, brushing my teeth, I am really disgusted"

After the body of Elisa was found, and due to the seemingly harmful quality of the water being supplied from the water tanks, tests were carried out. Water samples were taken from various places in the hotel. All tests came back negative for live bacteria that may be associated with Lam's body in the tank, and/or human waste. However, people from the environmental health went on to say "The testing we did was only looking for this coliform group of bacteria, but we really don't have much information about what occurred on previous days". The tests did not, therefore, take into account the condition of the water before the samples were taken.

On the Tuesday a "do not drink" warning was put in place and remained so over the weekend, until after public health authority deemed the water safe to drink, and use. Perhaps by co-incidence, the day after Lam went missing; there was a minor flood on the fourth floor. It is not known what caused this, but some believe there was "some obstruction to the drain between the third and fourth floor", that was caused by Elisa's body.

Whilst waiting for the results of the water test, Angelo Bellomo, of the environmental health, made a statement, saying "You don't always get the results that you expect after you implement the cleaning. In some cases, the cleaning and flushing process could shake loose other things in the system that creates contamination problems of their own. So we'll just have to wait and see what happens, but if the testing comes back good, then we would be placing the system back into operation". So, here he is explaining that if contamination is found in the water, it may or may not be due to the situation of Elisa's body in the water tank, contaminating the water supply. He was clearly informing the public that there are a number of possibilities. He went on to say that the lines and tanks will be flushed and sanitized in the very near future.

Whilst people were still staying in the hotel despite the finding of Lam's body and all of the investigations that were taking place, they were told to only use the water to flush the toilet. The Cecil provided bottled water for drinking and general use in the meantime. These guests were asked to sign waivers that stated that if they continue to use the water to drink, despite being advised not to, then the Cecil would not be held responsible for ill health caused. Now we shall look at the hotel itself, and its dark history.

The Cecil Hotel's history:

Although it seems like any ordinary hotel, the Cecil Hotel was actually very irregular place to stay. It was, and remains to be, a budget hotel and was built in 1924; there were originally 700 rooms. In the 1930s and 40s it was a grand destination for the rich and famous to stay-however it was not to remain so. It gradually deteriorated- just as the rest of "downtown" LA did, particularly in the notable skid row area. It subsequently attracted a more dubious type of customer.

One reason that the hotel did not "go under" completely, was because it offered very low prices and rates. However this meant that it attracted people who were very close to being homeless. The hotel was given a multi-million dollar refurbishment in 1997; however this did nothing to halt the ever increasing number of calls made to the police, to investigate matters of abuse in the hotel, and the use of narcotics by some of the patrons there. The hotel's sinister history includes two serial killers who stayed at the hotel- Richard Ramirez and Jack Unterweger.

Ramirez, in 1985 was staying on the top floor, and was nicknamed "The Night Stalker". He came from Texas and stayed at other hotels in the area, though he was charged just $14 per night at the Cecil and spent around a month and a half there. Due to the fact that the hotel was full of transients, it initially went unnoticed that Ramirez stalked and murdered women. There is evidence to suggest that following the murders, he got rid of the bloodied clothes and other incriminating evidence by putting them into a nearby dumpster, before entering the hotel through the back entrance. His crimes mainly took place in 1985, but not solely in or around the Cecil Hotel. In 1989 he was sentenced to death, after being found guilty of fourteen burglaries, 11 sexual assaults, 13 murders and 5 attempted murders. Despite being on death row for 23 years, he died of unrelated medical complications, in June 2013, aged 53 years old.

Jack Unterweger was another unrelenting criminal; whilst he resided at the Cecil Hotel, he was found to be responsible for killing three prostitutes. In 1974 he was convicted of murder but was later released early to begin rehabilitation. Though, after his released he began to murder again. Whilst staying at the Cecil Hotel, three prostitutes- Shannon Exley, Irene Rodriguez and Sherri Ann Long, were savagely beaten, before being sexually assaulted, and then brutally strangled with their own bras.

However, the hotel not only lodged these famous serial killers, it also became a hot spot for suicide. In the 1950s and 1960s, numerous suicides took place. In 1954, a guest called Helen Gurnee became the first documented suicide in the Cecil Hotel. She had jumped from a seventh floor window- she was killed outright when she landed on top of the hotel's marquee. It is possible that this suicide was planned, due to her registering in the hotel under the name of "Margaret Brown".

The second guest to commit suicide through jumping to her death, was Julia Moore. She had jumped out of her window on the eighth floor but what is puzzling, is the fact that when her hotel room was subsequently searched, the only things she left behind were: fifty nine cents change, a bank book (this showed a monetary balance of $1800), and the bus ticket that she used to get to LA.

Another disturbing example of this was the death, in 1962, of 27 year old Pauline Otton. After arguing with her husband, she threw herself out a ninth floor window. This is made doubly tragic due to the fact that she landed on top of a pedestrian- Mr George Gianni, 65. Both were killed instantly. Due to the strange circumstance, it was initially thought that both the victims were involved in a suicide pact but after later investigation the truth came out.

A couple of years later, there was a murder that still to this day, remains unsolved. A lady called Goldie Osgood, who was nicknamed "Pigeon Goldie" and "Pigeon Lady" due to her fondness of feeding birds in the surrounding areas, was found dead in her room at the Cecil Hotel. Her death was brutal; evidence shows that she was raped, strangled and stabbed. Her room was then ravaged by her assailant. After the crime took place, a 29 year old man, named Jacques.B.Ehlinger was seen walking through the same area of the park that "Pigeon Goldie" fed the pigeons. Apparently his clothes marked with blood- he was arrested for the murder but later cleared himself of the crime. Whether it be a pre-meditated murder, or a robbery gone wrong, we will probably never know. As so many of these violent, cruel and disturbing deaths have occurred in and around the Cecil Hotel, there is a chance that the death of Elisa Lam may also be linked to suicide or murder.

In 2010, a fire fighter named Charles Anthony MacDougall was stabbed at the Cecil Hotel on Main Street (it is unknown as to what reason the man, and a fellow fire fighter, were at the hotel). The perpetrator was never found and bizarrely MacDougall was said to have told his partner never to tell his significant other about the attack. There is very little available information about the attack, but it has been confirmed that it occurred around 10:50am, on May 18th, 2010. The fire fighter was upstairs in the hotel, whereas his partner was elsewhere. MacDougall said that the following occurred; he said he was inside the hotel's coffee shop, when he saw a man needed help to get up the stairs, trying to be helpful, he went to help the man, but as he was doing so, he was stabbed numerous times. Eventually MacDougall's partner went up the stairway to find his colleague heavily bleeding from his stab wounds.

The Cecil also had many long term residents as well as the ordinary day to day customers. Some of these people however, had "dodgy" pasts, and examples of this are rapists and drug addicts. One theory is that when the Cecil Hotel took new owners, they wished to bring a better, cleaner look and appearance to the Cecil. Did they then evict all the people that may tarnish the hotel's reputation? It would be very hard, considering their history, for these people to find new places to live, and this may have made them feel very bitter about the Cecil.

Therefore, did they wish to tarnish the hotel's reputation, by one or more of them murdering Lam, knowing that it would very much disgrace the Cecil Hotel? Thus nobody would want to stop at the hotel, and so the long term residents felt that they may once again, use the hotel as their abode.

Many people have strong opinions regarding the hotel and it is no secret that although some people enjoyed staying at the hotel due to its cheap rates, many people avoided staying there due to its dark history and atrocious location. There are many examples online, of people who are warning people against staying at the Cecil Hotel. One such example is an Expedia posting, saying:

"When I told my local LA friend where I was staying one night, giving this hotels address, I now understand his advice to find somewhere else ASAP" Another person posted an alarming review that said "You feel like you're gonna get knifed anytime". Even some travel agents were offering advice, saying that women travelling on their own should be careful. They should use "Ms" instead of "Miss" in bookings, should not advertise that they are single and should not answer the door unless they know who is on the other side.

On the day that Elisa's body was found, a South African lady called Pippa Beaumont, was seen rushing out of the Cecil, pulling her baggage along Main Street. She had not even had the chance to check in "I am a bit freaked out, I'm travelling alone" she said. On hearing about the finding of Lam's body, she told "I never would've thought".

A downtown resident that lived near the Cecil, Demetrius Wyman, upon seeing the posters of the then missing Lam, informed that "Its common for people to go missing around here, but not dead and missing, especially in a water tank". Then oddly, somebody posted on the internet "I live in the LA area, and I haven't heard a word about the investigation. The only news after the autopsy was about the water, and that was short lived. It's as if Elisa Lam never existed here". Does this imply that a cover up was in place or that there was something to hide, in some way?

Another internet user then said "LA is my hometown, and let me say A LOT of murders happen there and they never get reported on. It is such a large city and the news tends to be more centred on grabbing ratings than keeping the city informed". Was the case of Lam overshadowed by things in the media that were more "interesting to the public" or again, was the lack of information given about Lam, due to a cover up?

The area which the hotel is situated is known to be a rough area to reside in. Crimes committed there range from assault, rape and increasingly so; murder. Some people live in this area because they simply cannot afford to live anywhere else, and though the quality of life there is poor, they risk the chance of being a victim of serious crime.

Links with films and books:

There is a bizarre connection, along with a multitude of coincidences, between the case of Elisa Lam, and things that have cropped up in books, television and film, both before and after Lam's disappearance. Perhaps the most famous of these, is the Japanese horror movie "Dark Water". The film includes numerous similarities, and some people believe that this is because there is a direct and undeniable link between the film and the case of Elisa Lam. Dark Water includes a malfunctioning elevator, and a young female being found dead in a water tank on top of an apartment block. Also, people in the movie complain of getting "black water" from their taps-just like what had later occurred in the Cecil Hotel.

But the similarities did not stop there. The connections with the characters in the movie, proved very strange too. The lead character was named Dahlia…"Black Dahlia" was the nickname given to a woman named Elizabeth Short, who stayed at the Cecil Hotel in 1947, shortly before her brutal murder. A Los Angeles newspaper quoted "The Black Dahlia, Elizabeth Short is alleged in at least one book to have hung out at the Cecil and drank at the bar next door before she disappeared in 1947, though cultural historians Kim Cooper and Richard Schave, say that it is all just a rumour".

In the movie, Dahlia's daughter is named Cecilia; most people would agree that that is frighteningly similar to the "Cecil" Hotel. Yet more concurrences in the movie are as follows. Dahlia, upon moving into her new apartment block, notices dark, or murky, water dripping from her bathroom ceiling. After investigating further she comes to find out that a young girl (named Natasha Rimsky) had drowned in one of the apartment buildings rooftop water tanks. This turned the water dark, and almost black in colour, as is the case of the Elisa Lam mystery.

Near to the end of the film, the elevator in the building malfunctions. Did all these similarities occur by coincidence, or was Lam's death a ritualistic murder, mirrored from a hit Hollywood movie? Or did Lam see the film and tried to act it out, was she perhaps disturbed by it, in a way she was not aware of.

Although not at all associated with the modern day Cecil Hotel as we know it, or with what happened to Elisa Lam, but the hotel has appeared in numerous books and articles over its lifetime. The hotel seems to have been used to form the basis of a hotel that appears in Raymond Chandler's story "Nevada Gas". This is because the location of both the real hotel, and the fictional hotel, are almost identical, as are the descriptions of gangsters and such like that haunted and still haunt, the hotels. Whether these connections are purely coincidental or if there is something more sinister going on with the world's media, each person must form their own opinion, but this can only be made when we have delved into the case further.

The Aftermath:

Following the finding of Elisa Lam's body, the Cecil Hotel remained open. New guests were allowed to check into the hotel merely a few hours after the fire department had removed Lam's body from the water tank atop the roof. As previously mentioned- it was made compulsory that guests sign a waiver that said that if they became ill whilst staying at the hotel (through use of the still possibly contaminated water), then the responsibility does not fall on the hotel. The Cecil Hotel released a statement saying that "You do so at your own risk and peril". Also, guests who had already paid for their room were not to receive a refund if they decided to check out and stay in another hotel.

After the news of Elisa's death was made public, Facebook users posted comments that were both critical, and supportive. Some were even spiteful and utterly pointless. However, one compassionate post was: "Our hearts go out to you, Elisa. Whether you have been met with violence or drugged before being killed, someone or some people should be held responsible." And another said:

"Seriously someone must know what the hell happened to this poor girl" However some people had already made up their own minds about what actually happened to Elisa. Some were very malevolent, and some were down right nasty. The problem with these posts are that they were posted in the immediate aftermath of the finding of Lam's body; before any real information was made available to the public.

Some people have posted that they absolutely do not believe that the female in the elevator is even Elisa Lam. This is without any evidence other than that, as one person suggests, a persons profile from the front, can look very different to that from the side. Another person goes on to state that the only link between the lady in the elevator, and Elisa Lam, is that they are clearly both of Asian ethnicity. During the initial investigation, the police department went onto the roof. But what had led them there? And would a more thorough investigation of the roof, and the water tanks on it, have meant that Elisa's body was found more quickly, and thus her body would be in a more fit state to have her post mortem done.

LAPD scent dogs were used throughout the search; did a scent from inside the hotel lead the dogs to a fire escape or possibly to a door that led to the rooftop. However it is also possible that any scent or any evidence on the roof may have simply been "washed away" because weather reports state that there was heavy rain between the disappearance and the search of the roof.

Scent work in cones, this is where scent comes out of the body in a cone shape. Wind can affect this by blowing the cones and this may have confused or misled the police dogs on their initial search, and as aforementioned, water can do the same.

Media Coverage:

There was a lot of coverage of the case in the media; on television news reports, interviews and in the written press. One such release by the LA Times reports that a fellow resident in the hotel said that he heard a "tremendous noise" in the room above him on the night before Lam's disappearance. It was later found that Elisa Lam was indeed staying in the room above the claimant (named Bernard Diaz).

There was an extensive report on Chinese television, released by Commander Andrew Smith, of the Los Angeles Police Department. He stated that the coroner has officially said that there was no evidence of any trauma at all on Lam's body; and nothing to indicate that she was abused or injured in any way. He then went on to say that the police didn't believe that Elisa's body was concealed in any place prior to being placed in the tank (this perhaps indicates that the police department did initially believe there as foul play). Smith said that they believed that she was in the tank probably most of the time that she was missing.

Lastly, Smith went on to say that the water in the tank was very deep- around ten feet, and at the time of release, he said he did not know if she was found floating at the top, or resting on the bottom of the tank. He concluded saying "but a body at the bottom of the tank would be difficult to see". Another theory is that Lam was being followed, and then entered the elevator, which consequently failed to work. A person had approached from an upper floor, or the roof, and approaches from the left. This mystery person tells Lam to exit the elevator and raise her hands, so that she can be searched. Somebody else then approaches from the right (perhaps with innocent intentions- to use the toilet maybe). Lam is then able to re enter the elevator due to the following person being distracted. The reason that we do not see the "follower" is perhaps because they are aware that there are cameras in the elevator.

When the door then fails again to close, Lam exits the elevator and is grabbed by someone or something. The aforementioned "innocent" person makes a re-appearance and, scared, Lam makes gestures to them, possibly asking for help, the person fails to respond and so Elisa is whisked away.

Was she responsible for her own death?

Most of the theories surrounding this case seem to centre around the fact that it was somebody else murdered her, or that her death was accidental. But there is another theory- that she was responsible for her own death. Did

27

Elisa stop taking her prescribed medication? (Possibly but unlikely, as there were traces of them in her tests). Had she taken street drugs, that made her so disorientated that she found herself on the rooftop, and climbed into the tank? These are said to be 90% of the cause. The 9% of the likely cause is that she befriended a person, possibly a drug user, and they somehow ended up on the roof, Lam may have overdosed and panicking, the other person found the most convenient place to dispose of the body was in the nearest water tank. The remaining 1% probability is that she was murdered by serial murderer who may have gotten her on the rooftop by using a threat of some sort, then abused her, before forcing her in the tank. All of these theories have little or no evidence to support them, and although interesting, they are simply speculations.

A similar case & The "Smiley Faced Killer"

In 2011, in a water tank atop a building, a maid's body was found. The rooftop was only supposed to be accessible by authorised personnel. But these such "authorised personnel" may include workers, sub contractors etc. The manager of the town council of the place where this took place said "there are no foolproof methods to prevent water tanks being sabotaged". On a Monday morning, residents in a block of apartments discovered that their water from their taps was a strange colour and was quite "frothy". This meant that the water tanks were then inspected, and subsequently the maid's body was found. However as with the Lam case, it is unknown when the body ended up in the tank.

During investigations it was found to be at least 40 accidental drowning, that were believed to be the work of one killer. These people appear to be drugged and all appear on CCTV sometimes before their deaths. Somebody who witnessed the video on a popular video website, commented "I believe that it has a lot to do with staff who were befriended by that guy he stayed enough at the hotel to be friends with staff and he really has a morbid way of talking about oriental girls. He has been known to party up on the top of the hotel rooftop. He could have lured this woman up there. I know these are assumptions but he was staying at the hotel at the same time Elisa was staying there" This was written by an anonymous person, so cannot be verified or checked and so must be put down to opinions and hypothesises.

The aforementioned information given about the young men found dead in water, were not accidental deaths, according to two New York City investigators. Instead, they were victims of the "Smiley Faced Killer". He was nicknamed such because in numerous places where his possible victims were found, there was smiley faces painted next to the body, or nearby.

Initial autopsy news:

Before the autopsy information was released, and opinions suggested, the following vague information is what was contained on the initial press release. It does not seem to assign suicide to the death of Lam, even though her bi-polar issues are mentioned at some point. However, accidental death does not seem to explain what happened either. This is because; how would Lam have gotten on top of a roof (which was, or should have been, locked), and then managed to open and manage to squeeze into a water tank. Whilst in the tank she may have felt her clothes were weighing her down, and so in a panic, stripped her own clothes off? But why, if she could have peered into the tank before climbing in, she would have seen that she would have seen that she would almost certainly not have been able to get back out.

The Autopsy Report:

Much of the information required to formulate an idea or opinion regarding this mystery, can be found in the autopsy report. The autopsy report includes a wealth of information including her physical appearance after death, information on her toxicology report, suggestions about how she died; and the coroner's final opinion/ verdict.

Her clothing:

Regarding Lam's clothes, there are a few peculiarities. When discovered, Lam was naked, and her clothes were found floating in the water near her. Lam's clothing was comprised of: a pair of black men's shorts, a large green shirt which had a logo on the back of the neck labelled "Alexander Keith's India Pale Ale". The shirt also had a logo of a deer on the front chest. Her sandals were also in the tank; they were black, with polka dots and were a size 39. She was also found with a red hooded sweatshirt with a zipped front, size extra small. When found, Lam's underpants- black, with lace trim and labelled Calvin Klein, were found in the tank also.

However, some of the clothing found with her and the clothing that she is wearing in the elevator video is intended for males. It is understood that some people feel more comfortable in larger, baggier clothes, but some of the items of clothing that she was wearing/found with, was intriguingly rather large indeed. Also, due to Lam knowing she was going to be travelling for a long while, why would she pack these clothes?

We do not know whether Lam climbed into the tank intentionally or whether she was forced there. If she took them off herself, it would make more sense if she did so before climbing into the water tank. However if she removed them in a panic- why did she strip completely naked including her underwear? Curiously, she was wearing her watch when found, and her key card, does this imply that she had left her room by her own volition and had a purpose in doing so- perhaps she did not intend to be gone for long? However her phone was never found. Was this because she had lost it, as she had previously said?

The mysterious "White Particles"

All of the clothing had white sand like particles attached to them, and the drying mats had them too. This was never fully investigated, though most agree that it should have been. If it was inspected properly, it could well have shown its origin. So we can only conclude that it was either from somewhere on the rooftop (that got stuck onto her shoes/feet), or in her sandals, or more likely was it already in the water and just became adhered to her clothes. If the investigation of the powder had been properly examined, it may have given evidence that could have changed the outcome of the case.

Lam's Physical Examination:

It is thought that Lam may have had an underlying medical condition, possibly a thyroid disorder. Upon completing the autopsy it was found that there are issues with Lam's thyroid that are not consistent with decomposition- thus she did have thyroid problems before death. She may not have been aware of this, as she was not taking medication for it, and it is not unheard of that people with thyroiditis have no symptoms at all. The disease is quite common for women; it is said that around 40% of females are found to have focal thyroiditis found in autopsy.

If Elisa had climbed, rather riskily over the pipes and the sharp corners of the rim of the hatch into the small opening, it would be most likely that she would have some sort of contusions, grazing, cuts etc, but she did not seem to have any of these things that would concur with climbing into the tank.

The external examination of Elisa's body showed up numerous indicators. Lam's features show that she appeared to be her actual age, of 21. She was a slim young lady, weighing 121 pounds, had a small insignificant scar on her right knee, and a tiny abrasion on her left knee. There were no wrist scars or other evidence of self harm, and Lam had no tattoos on her body.

Her head was what is called "normocephalic", which simply means that it was the normal shape and size for a girl of her age. Her hair was straight and brown with no signs of balding and her eyes were also brown, with no haemorrhages. Lam had no missing teeth and no dentures. Her neck, abdomen and chest were all normal and unremarkable, as was her genitalia. Her limbs did not show any oedema, abnormalities or deformities. Notably there were no needle punctures on her body.

Internal Examination:

Generally Elisa's body was in an average state of decomposition, and her feet/lower legs showed signs of slight greening along with a slightly marbled appearance on her thighs. Her scalp and hair, when slightly plucked, came away effortlessly. Lam's eyes were noted to be bulging and her face and head slightly bloated. Slippage is present on her cheeks and forehead. (Slippage is where a corpse's skin, nails and hair start to loosen and "slip off" after death). This was also present on the back, chest, arms and lower legs. Lam's palms and soles of her feet were somewhat wrinkled.

There were no signs of trauma on Elisa's neck, and nothing out of the ordinary relating to her lips, gums or teeth. Soft tissues were taken from her larynx, but this showed no signs of haemorrhage; her hyoid bone is also in tact. Samples of thyroid cartilage that were taken were also unremarkable. Because of her body decomposing, the tissues of the abdominal walls had become discoloured somewhat, and softened. There was no damage or irregularities to her breasts, and all of her organs in the abdominal cavity were unremarkable and normally arranged. There were no deformities to her bony framework or muscles.

The cardiovascular system seemed completely normal. Her aorta showed no signs of atherosclerosis, and no aneurisms present. Lam's heart was entirely healthy, and the chambers within it had developed normally. In Lam's respiratory passages, secretions were found and the mucosa had a brownish discolouration, which is normally post-mortem.

Her gastrointestinal system was in tact, her stomach was not distended, and her intestines were all normal. It should be noted that at this point, no tablets were found in Lam's stomach.

Elisa's hepatobiliary system, which includes the liver and gallbladder were normal, as was her urinary system, which contains her bladder and kidneys. Next, her genital system was investigated, and there was no trauma present in the vaginal wall or around the cervix, and all parts of this system were normal in appearance, except for a slight discolouration of her vagina. Her ovaries were completely normal for a girl of her age.

Her eyes and her inner ear were never dissected as it was decided at the time that this was not necessary. Regarding the head and nervous system; her scalp was not haemorrhaged, there was no skull fracture and her brain was soft and normally coloured and showed no cerebral contusions. Her spinal cord was also not dissected.

Toxicology Reports

During the autopsy a screen of her bile, heart blood, brain, spleen, stomach contents and liver tissue were requested. Ed Winter, a coroner's office spokesperson said "Toxicology tests must be performed on the body of Elisa Lam to determine if she was taking medication or another substance". Results from her heart blood, showed that she was taking the following medication, and results from her liver showed that she was taking prescribed medicines also.

Lam's Prescribed Medications:

When these tests were carried out they discovered that she was in fact, taking a number of prescribed medications. Lam was taking Advil, which is a pain killer (10mg), Lamotrigine, which can be used to treat Bipolar disorder (100mg), and quetiapine, which can also be used to treat bipolar disorder, along with other mental health issues (25mg). As well as these, Lam was also prescribed venlafaxine, which is an antidepressant (150mg, 4x daily) and wellbutrin- another antidepressant (300mg). Found within her possessions were: a pill cutter, three pill cases, and prescription receipts. It would be concluded that Lam certainly had some diagnosed mental illness that she did not disclose to people, despite her family having some idea that she was struggling mentally. She most likely wanted to keep her illness, or ill mental health, to herself and medical professionals.

Were Illicit Drugs Involved?

The video of Lam in the elevator shows her acting very strangely, and some would say that it was the behaviour of somebody under the influence of illegal drugs. An expert on drugs viewed the footage and stated "it's hard to say" whether Lam was under the influence. She seems to be petting or stroking something and at one point appears to do a little dance. These are symptoms/indications of a person who has taken, for example, ecstasy; this contains hallucinogens and MDMA. Her behaviour seems to be fuelled by paranoia, and it can be said that she was hallucinating at times, due to taking such strong illicit drugs. However, if it could be proved that the whole course of events was initially sparked by drugs, it would not be able to prove whether she took the drugs voluntarily or was forced to take them.

Porrata, the specialist that was investigating the case, said that people under the influence of ecstasy, often wonder around, and end up in "strange places". However she then went on to say that climbing into a water tank atop a roof was not typical behaviour of a person who had taken an "E". Porrata, who has worked on cases similar to Lam's, admitted that the rooftop was a very strange place to end up. "People under the influence of PCP, may like going near water. It does have a tendency to attract people to water".

So do these things indicate that drugs had caused Lam's death in some way? Probably not- the theories do not concur with the lab test results, which showed no sign of these illicit drugs in her system.

A random theory which has since been found to not be true (due to lab results), is that she took an overdose in or around the tank and died in the tank, perhaps she did this so that nobody can find and resuscitate her.

If Lam had taken drugs and/or alcohol (again, this was disproved) she may have been accidently drowned by climbing in the tank and inhaling water which would have killed her. But still- why would she get in the tank? Was it because she had mental health issues or was it due to being inebriated?

If you were in Elisa Lam's situation (whatever that is), and she really did feel the need, and had the means to, immerse yourself in a water tank. It may go as follows. You would need to climb to the top of the tank and open the lid (details surrounding the tank and lid are to follow), put your legs in the opening and sit on the ledge. Next, feeling the water level with your feet, you edge your bottom off the ledge, holding one hand on the edge and one to pull the lid closed. Then you would lower yourself, before letting go and falling into the tank. You would then realise that there was no way out.

It was found that Lam' body was found floating in the water feet up with her head pointing down. The official FBI website says that this is the way that drowning victims become orientated. Did parts of the skin or body start to clog the pipes which would lead to the poor water quality issues? Rather disgustingly, the FBI website also states that the skin of people who have drowned can slip off like a glove. So, it is not known if there was any turbulence in a water tank, and is the pipe suction powerful? Would it be strong enough to make a body move around and turned about.

The tank itself:

We know very little information about the tank itself, but what we do know, proves crucial to the investigation. The American Water Works Association says that there should have been a ladder that would make the tanks more accessible (for maintenance etc). The old age of the hotel Cecil also made it exempt from new lids being fitted on top of the tanks.

Interestingly the lid is hinged, and it can only ever been open or closed; never half open, as there is no mechanism to allow this. It is unlikely, some say, that the lid would be off because the lids should be sealed shut to keep out foreign objects- LAPD officer Smith suggested that the lids were not locked but they were closed. If Lam climbed into the tank herself she would have had to hold the lid open with one hand, and attempt to lower herself into the tank with the other hand. This may be possible but would require immense strength (did Lam have such strength?), and finally, would Elisa know that the lid would close behind her if she was inside.

What else could have been investigated?

There was a great deal of media coverage that arose surrounding the mystery of Elisa Lam. However, like many stories like Elisa's that have a lot of coverage, there are people who take it upon themselves to do some investigations of their own. Some people had the following ideas that they believe should be carried out independently of legitimate enquiries:

- Examine the 14th floor fire escape, which is believed to be where Elisa would have used if she had independently made her way onto the roof top.

- Find out what room Elisa stayed in (as this was not released until later on in the investigation)

- To prove that the roof top door was locked at the time of Elisa being found in the tank, it would be essential to attempt to open the door, just for evidence.

- To see what it would have been like if Elisa was on the roof top at night, it would be fruitful to stay overnight at the Cecil, and judging on whether the roof is accessible, explore the roof at night.

- Suggesting for one moment that Elisa's body was carried up to the roof, perhaps, someone suggested, that somebody should try carrying a large suitcase up the fire escape and into the water tank to see if it is possible.

- Next attempt to discuss with occupants who have rooms of the 14th and 15th floors, to see whether they heard or saw anything, or have any further suggestions.

- Some people believe that one of the reasons that the water from the hotel to the tank was discoloured and with poor pressure, is because an item of clothing, (or body part) got stuck inside of a pipe. So it would be prudent to try and examine the size of the pipe to see if something such as a sandal could have got stuck in it.

These are just a few of the suggestions people have put forward. It is unknown whether anybody actually acted on these ideas, but they are interesting nonetheless.

Depression and her blogs:

It was no secret that Elisa Lam was a keen blogger. It was clear from what she wrote in these blogs, that she was suffering some form of depression. She openly writes "I had a relapse at the start of the term and I had to drop 2 or 3 of the courses I was taking. Now I am down to one course and I have missed 3 weeks of classes since my sleep pattern is completely reversed". And in another she writes "Depression sucks. I have no control over my emotions. I will be angry for two minutes and then sad again. I will be happy for half an hour and then emotional again." In the final police report it states that her depression got so severe that it resulted in bipolarity that then resulted in her climbing to the top of a 10 ft water tank, removing her clothes, and getting in. Either she fell in, or this is a case of suicide. Whether she made her way to the roof herself and whether she freely got into the tank, is not in question. What is being stated here is the fact that she almost certainly was suffering some form of mental illness.

On Reddit.com, a social networking site a friend of Lam's posted "I don't know exactly what kind of mental problems she had, but I and her close friends know that she had some strange episodes before and she has disappeared before too. However her family was always reluctant to talk about her problems, like in this case where they refused to release any information regarding her mental problems. Once we found out that she was going through some therapy for three weeks and has regular depressions. I didn't talk to her for a year so I didn't know why she was going to LA. I suspect it is connected to schizophrenia or some mental problems rather than recreation drug use. She was travelling alone and it is suspicious too".

Lam continued to post on her blog, which was named "Ether Fields". Though most of her earlier postings were about general things, such as what an ordinary young woman would post about, some of her later posts were more alarming and thought provoking. I will focus on five of these posts that show that she was most likely suffering mental illness.

The first "On Happiness", 24.11.11. "Happiness in intelligent people is the rarest thing I know" She appears to be hinting of her own depression and possibly saying that she thinks of herself as intelligent. In her opening paragraph she speaks of a "bitch of a friend"...had she suffered a falling out? (Remembering that this was posted in 2011), and if so was it a close friend? Did the falling out last until the time of Elisa's death? She also says that she did not class this friend as intelligent.

It becomes obvious that Lam was suffering some sort of depression when she says: "I would bet a great deal of money that no one is happy and everyone is intelligent in their way" It is possible that she was thinking in this way because she in herself, was very unhappy and couldn't understand how anybody in this life, can possibly be truly happy. Elisa goes on to say that if a person is intelligent or an over-thinker, they are unable to process happiness and sadness. It seems that her basic line of thinking can be generalised by saying that if a person is intelligent they can see with clarity but also they can see the negatives in day to day living. It is this potential seeing the "bad" in things that means they can become their own worst enemies.

The cleverer a person is, it says, the fewer the amount of people they believe they can talk to as equals. The quote suggests also, that moderately intellectual people are able to be content and happy with the world that they live in. In another quote from one of her blogs she states that she feels she cannot process her thoughts effectively and finds it difficult to put her thoughts into words. Elisa said on tumblr that she finally feels she has found people (on tumblr) that share the same issues and problems as herself.

The aforementioned quotes were written on or before November 2011. Her latest quote of that time was "I simply have no motivation to do anything, let alone leave my bed". This seems to suggest that indeed she was depressed- at some point in her life anyway. However, did her depression subside? As she clearly had gained some motivation in order to go travelling...or was this just a front and really, mentally, she was still in turmoil? Even back then she admitted that her online activity was a lifeline to her and this was backed up by her regular blogs- some about mundane day to day life, and others surrounding subjects that went a little deeper. She felt that she could say anything on the internet, and she would be understood because there is always somebody out there who is thinking and feeling the same. Lam says, regarding the internet, "people cannot judge you on your good looks and clothing and you feel less pressured"...she went on to say that she felt that any five minutes that she spent online, was more "spectacular" than any five minutes of her real life.

It is unknown whether she was a victim of online bullying/stalking. In one blog she says "...and then you find out they're creeping you and you go gah they know all these intimate details and the innermost thoughts of the people in know! Don't find me in real life!" One person who commented on a post of Lam's divulged that they too suffered depression. Did this person know Lam personally and so knew she was depressed? Or was it s obvious from Elisa's blogs that she was blatantly depressed and was so obviously "fighting demons" that she may or may not have been getting treatment for. The person seems to be reaching out to Lam, saying "feel free to email if you want someone to chill/ talk with".

In 2012 Lam posted numerous pieces of information that would indicate that she was suffering. These include "I had a relapse at the start of the term and had to drop two or three courses I was taking"..."My sleeping pattern is completely reversed"..."I am a bit defeated, I have no one

46

to spend time with"..."I have very little going on in my life, which is disappointing"..."I'm very disappointed in myself, so utterly directionless and lost".

Bizarrely, after this, her mental health and her direction in life started to "pick up". She states in her Etherfields blog in March 2012 that "things are going fairly well". She seems to acknowledge that she was depressed when she says "I believe the biggest reason why I got depressed was..." However her mood seems to dip again, when in April 2012 she writes a blog titled "Worries of a twenty something". She wrote things in this blog, such as:

"I don't know how to do anything...I'll be judged...I can't do it...I can't do it alone" and thinking to herself "You're so lazy you will never accomplish anything... you are a phony...why are you such a snob?!" This post sparked many people to comment on it, including:

"You really need to speak to someone in real life about what you are going through." And, rather harshly, someone says "This will seem stupid to many people, because I am writing to a dead person". Another one of Elisa's blogs was titled "Expecto Patronum", and was written in November of the same year. She begins "I have no control over my emotions, I will be happy for half and hour and then emotional again". So, is this a usual response to ordinary life events, or possibly a sign of mental illness? Bipolar disorder perhaps. She went on to say that she is being "candid" about her depression, because she felt she would feel less alone if she knew that someone in the same position as her, read her posts.

Lam completely fits the profile a person leading a double life. She was connecting with people online, was isolating herself, and was depressed. Was she beginning to have paranoid thoughts and behaviours? She knew that she was saying things in her blogs that would frustrate or upset people and was scared that there "would be crazies out there googling me".

Was Lam suffering a Psychotic Break?

We know that Elisa had mental health issues, but was she psychotic? If she was, it is possible that she was having a psychotic episode that led to a series of events that ultimately, led to her death. However, if a person was having a psychotic break, the aforementioned natural instinct, when submerged in water, would still kick in. But, did she end up in the tank due to a break in reality, become immersed, and simply failed to climb back out?

If so, exhaustion or panic may have led to her drowning. However if she was physically fighting to find her way to the top, and out of the tank, there should have been physical signs of this; contusions or bruising for example.

Was Elisa afraid of something and felt that she needed to seek refuge somewhere? Suggesting for a second that she had managed to get onto the roof, and then succeeded in opening the tank, could she have climbed in, only to have the lid close on her, and leaving her in a psychotic state, and unable to free herself from the tank. If Lam was suffering such psychosis, did she become trapped on the roof? This could have been a suggestion because the fire door to the roof only opens from the inside...the only way off the roof is down the fire escape.

Some people who are suffering psychosis feel the need to be near or around water- but if this was the case with Elisa, why didn't she stand in a shower? Or if she was looking for somewhere to hide, why didn't she hide in a wardrobe? And if she was hiding (from something) she did a good job, because she evaded detection until the LAPD found her body a number of weeks later. Another view is that if a person suffered from paranoia, they would most likely try to avoid being in enclosed spaces, so why would she use the roof as a point of refuge?

Strangulation? Or perhaps drowning?

Strangulation is a difficult issue, because there can sometimes be no external evidence of it whatsoever. However there can still be markings internally, for example contusions on the neck muscles, or fractured hyoid bone. Though some people contest this, the focal erythema of the thyroid- which is what was found in Elisa's case, is not a sign of a person being strangled.

As a general rule it is very complicated to prove that drowning is a cause of death. Drowning is described as "… a form of asphyxia due to aspiration of fluid into the air passages, caused by submersion in water/other fluid. Complete submersion is not necessary, for submersion of the nose and mouth alone for a sufficient period can cause death from drowning".

Suicide by drowning is very rare because breathing is a primal function- your brain and body would always fight against it. A quote to describe this is "Suicide by drowning is the act of deliberately submerging oneself in water or other liquid to prevent breathing and deprive the brain of oxygen. Due to the body's natural tendency to come up for air, drowning attempts often involve the use of a heavy object to overcome this reflex". In Elisa's case, no heavy object was found in the water tank, so if she had wanted to drown herself, she clearly had not thought it completely through. However we do know that Elisa's body was found floating in the water with her feet pointing up, and her head pointing down. According to information supplied by the FBI, this is the natural way that victims of drowning become accustomed.

Interesting things to know:

There are lots of curiosities surrounding this case, and a lot of things that would be interesting to know. We do not know the exact time of the video and the precise time that she disappeared. What experiences did any of the other hotel residents have with Lam and is it at all possible that she was sleep walking? Does she have a history of this, or has anybody ever seen her do this? It would be interesting to know also, what kind of strength would it take to open the tank's lid? Would it take considerable strength, or would a slight person, like Elisa, be able to do it unaided? Why didn't the team of officers that went on to the roof open the other tanks too...might there have been other bodies?

Next it has been reported that the hotel had water pressure problems for a long time before the case of Elisa Lam. Other reasons that made the water pressure yet more significant may be because the decomposition of her body caused parts of her body to become clogged in the exit pipes, or perhaps was it her clothes that got sucked into the pipes, blocking them.

Was Elisa Lam becoming objectified?

Yes, it could be said that Elisa Lam had been completely objectified since the finding of her body in 2013. She is known as the corpse behind the whole scandal; this is very off-putting, even for the hardiest of people. And why was she turned from being the cute Canadian missing girl, into the creepy, weird girl. This was almost solely due to the release of the strange video footage. Did this dehumanise Lam? It is hard to decide whether Lam simply had no friends that were willing to talk to the media or if the media just did not put any effort into investigating this area. In the early stages of the case, the public became annoyed at the lack of information that was being released to them. However, there was no cause for this because in fact, there was no real information to give out. To start with the media then clung on to the only aspect that had any decent amount of facts and certainty; the water quality.

Confirmation Bias:

According to The Skeptics Dictionary, Confirmation Bias is a psychological, scientific term that "refers to a type of selective thinking whereby one tends to notice and look for what confirms ones beliefs and to ignore, not look for, or undervalue the relevance of what contradicts ones beliefs". The case if Elisa Lam is a prime example of this-how the brain attempts to fill in details and seek evidence of what that person wants to be true. This means that when people watch the video of Elisa in the elevator, people's brains start to erase logical explanations that may explain Lam's behaviour and instead looks for paranormal phenomenon, where one almost certainly does not exist. The death of Lam and her behaviour may actually be able to be explained rationally and there are many possibilities for it...all of which occur naturally.

A less likely theory:

Here is a much less likely theory yet, as with other theories, it should be scrutinised. It may be that somebody knows exactly what happened and are keeping it quiet. This may be a person who had connections with her, or had a friend, that ultimately killed her. Though initially investigated, it was explored no more, as the media did not give it any more attention; however the Chinese media bizarrely did, to some extent. So we know that Lam was 21, was attending university, and went travelling. But people are refusing to talk about Lam's family life/friends/upbringing. One reason that we do not know much about these things is because she had a very private family, and possibly there may be cultural issues involved.

Yet another theory is this: Perhaps Elisa was already on the roof (for whatever reason), encountered a suspect and then began to feel slightly ill. She took the stairs off the roof, and became and scared. She went into the hall to try and find her room, via the elevator. The said elevator was broken; so the suspect could have caught up with Lam in the hallway- they realised she must be in the elevator. But the suspect knew that there was CCTV in there, so they knew they must not enter or walk past the elevator. Unfortunately, the whole hotel only had a small number of CCTV cameras.

Another strange idea is the following. Tuberculosis (TB) is becoming a big issue in downtown LA's tramp population (this in the area that the Cecil Hotel was in. At the time of Elisa's death there was an outbreak in the area, nothing remarkable there? Take into account that the new diagnostic test to TB is called...The Lam Elisa Test (!). Some people make a big issue out of this, and others think it is either untrue, or a huge coincidence.

Strange coincidences:

The case of Elisa Lam, and all the facts, opinions and views surrounding the mystery, has a bizarre, and some would say alarming number of coincidences and twists of fate. There are coincidences around Elisa herself, her travels, the Cecil Hotel, and also around what happened before, during and after her disappearance and consequently, her death.

Elisa was a regular blogger, and in one of her blogs, Elisa mentioned of a zombie survival game called "Left For Dead". The game is based around a fictional city, in which a person escapes from sewer pipes on the roof of a building- this was similar in ways, to Elisa's case. After Lam's discovery in February 2013, there have been two more cases of females, of around Lam's age, being found dead; water is involved in both of these other cases. The first of these young girls was found in early March in California- her name was Tina Hoang; she was found face down, dead, on a beach. She was facing charges for prostitution at the time (this differs from Elisa's case, as she was not knowingly facing charges of any kind). Her death was suspicious and because of her association with men who meet escorts, it is ever more possible that Tina had been drugged before being drowned.

The other woman was (who is unnamed) was found dead in the water at a surfing point in Santa Barbara. At the time, this woman was not being investigated for any criminal matters. The coincidences here are that they were all young females, and it is not determined whether there was any foul play regarding their deaths, or whether they are simply a series of misfortunes that led to these deaths. They were all found in the beginning of the month, and all involved water.

There are other coincidences too, surrounding her name. The following days after Lam's body was found, there was a suspected outbreak of a strain of tuberculosis amongst vagrants in the downtown area, near the Cecil Hotel. What is extremely bizarre about this is that the diagnosis test for this strain of TB, (that is undertaken by using sputum and urine samples), is called the Lam-Elisa test.

The strangest coincidence in the case was perhaps the Crowley-Elisa connection. A writer named Aleister Crowley wrote a poem in the late eighteen hundreds, whilst staying at the Cecil Hotel. He called the poem Jephthah. There are a number of similarities: in the poem Jephthah had a daughter named Seila…which is a perfect anagram for "Elisa". Some of the lines and verses in the poem seem to connect or have some likeness to Elisa Lam, and things that surrounded her case.

Firstly, one of the lines is "Let my lamp, at midnight hour". Some would say that this has a link purely because the word Lam appears somewhere within it (Let my LAMp…) Another states "Been seen in some highly tower", so, this seems to concur with Lam's body being found on the rooftop of the Cecil. What seems to be quite sinister is that further on in the poem, Crowley wrote "…her mansion in the fleshy nook". A "nook" is described as "a corner or recess, especially one offering seclusion". Many people believe that the water tank that Lam's body was found in, could definitely be described as "a nook". A final part of the poem says "some time let gorgeous tragedy". The death of Elisa Lam can absolutely, no matter what theories or ideas have been suggested, be called a tragedy.

The poem was written over a hundred years before the disappearance and death of Elisa Lam. So, unless Crowley had some strange powers of prediction, the similarities between poem and Lam, is almost certainly a series of pure coincidences.

The Final Police Report:

The USA Today stated that the final police report ruled that Lam's death was purely accidental and also that she suffered from bipolar disorder. Online reports seem to push aside the fact that she may (or actually may not) have mental illness, and focus instead on that there were no drugs in her system, nor was she known to take drugs.

(Again, this is an example of confirmation bias- omitting the possibility of her having a mental illness and focuses on her non-drug-use).

Next, police reports also state that the tank which Lam was found submerged in had "unlocked openings". With regards to these water tanks, the media instead focussed on the fact that the tank was behind a "locked and alarmed door that only employees had the key to", rather than paying attention to the fact that the actual water tank was unlocked. Erased information here is that the tank could be reached by climbing a (unlocked) fire escape. This is very accessible and easy to climb, especially by a twenty one year old woman.

Final Coroners verdict:

The witnesses to the autopsy were named as Detective Wallace Tennelle, and Stearns. The verdict is as follows. It was decided that Elisa Lam died by drowning. No sign of trauma was found on her body at all, and toxicology reports found that there was no significant alcohol or drug intoxication. Whilst investigating, they found that Elisa did indeed have a history of bipolar disorder and was prescribed medication for it (it was clear that some, but not all, of her close friends and family were aware of this). After reviewing all circumstances, it was concluded that Elisa did not intend to harm herself. Thus, it is said "The manner of death is classified as accident".

The report stated "At 17:21 hours, I observed the decedent, an adult female, lying on a service table...She was nude and her clothing items were with her on the table".

He then went on to say (which has been covered earlier), that she was in an advanced stage of decomposition, how she had been found and in what position, and also the fact that there was several dark hairs/fibres found on two or three of her garments.

Samples of Lam's fingernails, hair and pubic hair were taken, and a sexual abuse evidence kit was used. The coroner investigator, finally released Lam's hotel key and watch to the police department, and the report and investigations concluded at 18:50.

Physical evidence was collected also, using a sexual assault evidence kit, and a fingernail kit. Her clothing was also examined, and as aforementioned it contained amongst other things, a pair of sandals, a hooded sweater and black underwear.

The report states that at approximately 12:49 on the 19th of February, the death of Elisa was reported to the LA police department's Robbery & Homicide Division.

The verdict says that Lam had travelled alone from Vancouver and had arrived in Los Angeles on the 26th of January 2013. It then states that CCTV in the elevator shows Lam acting quite bizarrely, and though there were no other people in the frame, she seems to be in some sort of distress. The video depicted Elisa wearing the clothes that were found with her in the water tank.

At around 10:00 on the morning of 19th of February, a maintenance worker was sent on to the roof top to investigate guests' complaints about the water pressure and colour in the hotel. It was then that Elisa Lam's body was found in one of the large water tanks. The fire and police departments were called immediately and her death was confirmed at 10:22.

To conclude the report, it is stated that the possible place of injury is: Cecil Hotel, 640s Main Street, LA, 90014. And that the place the body was found was in a water tank atop the hotel.

The coroners report gives us many details surrounding different areas of Lam's mysterious death. However, it should not all be taken as fact. This is because not all of the information can be clarified and after the corners written and autopsy were complete, more information has come to light and other theories have been formed. We will look at these in the following chapters.

To conclude...

Lam's behaviour in the elevator can certainly be described as strange, and some say "not human", however, it looks exactly like the behaviour of a person who is experiencing mania or confusion. So, how can her death be explained? Firstly, she is not the only person to have ever drowned in a water tank, in 2010 in New Jersey a man climbed into a water tank, and drowned (this was classed as suicide). Also, in 2013, a toddler died in a water tank....these are only two examples, there are many more.

Each and every part of Lam's death can be explained naturally. It tarnishes her memory (and the fact that she clearly struggled mentally) to start creating wacky and obscure theories about paranormal experiences, murders and other bizarre ideas. Perhaps it is at this point that we should draw a line under the case.

She may or may not have been seriously mentally ill, and she may or may not have climbed into the tank herself due to a psychotic break. Or she may even have been assaulted and/or murdered. There may even have been something paranormal happening, but the fact is that...we may never know exactly what happened to her. For every theory there are facts that may prove it correct, or incorrect. For now let us simply preserve the memory of Elisa Lam (RIP).

Elisa Lam- The Mystery

On January 26th 2013, Elisa Lam, a Chinese-Canadian tourist checked into the Cecil Hotel in Los Angeles. Just five days later, she mysteriously disappeared, leaving no evidence or clues as to where she had gone or what had happened to her. The last sighting of Elisa alive was in the hotel lobby, sometime on January 31st. Following her sudden disappearance, and upon realising that she was a missing person, the LA police department launched a man hunt and investigations began.

Several days later, her body was found in a water tank situated on the roof of the Cecil Hotel. Her death, and the situations surrounding it, are highly suspicious, and it has sparked hundreds of theories and conspiracies from people around the globe. Was it murder? Or perhaps suicide? Or was something more out of the ordinary to blame- something paranormal? I have researched this case thoroughly, and in this book I am to detail the most popular theories, information and facts surrounding this most bizarre mystery.

Although there seems to be countless theories, ideas and speculations surrounding the mystery of Elisa Lam, and her death, there are many facts that we do know that are undoubted and certain. Elisa Lam was a Canadian tourist, of Chinese descent. She was a slight young woman of around a hundred and fifteen pounds, and standing at five feet, four inches tall. She was well educated, and was fluent in English and Cantonese Chinese.

Elisa left her home in January 2013, to begin what she called her "West Coast Tour". She had planned to visit San Diego, Los Angeles, Santa Cruz and San Francisco, though her travels were to go no further than Los Angeles. During her time travelling, she was noted to have used many forms of transport, such as buses and trains, and seemed confident in doing so. Everything appeared well up until the point of after arriving in Los Angeles. Lam had posted pictures of herself at the San Diego zoo, where she looked happy, content, and untroubled.

Elisa had arrived in LA on January 26th and checked herself into the Cecil Hotel. It appears that she was not put off by the hotels openly sinister history. Throughout her travels, Elisa had kept regular contact with her family and so, when they had not heard from her on January 31st, they began to worry, and thus contacted the Los Angeles police department. The family immediately flew to LA to assist in the search for Elisa. A missing person report was officially filed on 4/2/13, and this stated that she was last seen, at the Cecil Hotel, on 31/1/13. Lam had been travelling alone and had arrived in LA on 26/1/13.